LENNY WILKENS

JASON TERRY

LOU HUDSON

MOOKIE BLAYLOCK

DOMINIQUE WILKINS

BOB PETTIT

STEVE SMITH

CLIFF HAGAN

DOC RIVERS

PETE MARAVICH

DAN ROUNDFIELD

DIKEMBE MUTOMBO

CREATIVE C EDUCATION
JOHN NICHOLS

Published by Creative Education, 123 South Broad Street, Mankato, MN 56001

Creative Education is an imprint of The Creative Company.

Design and Art Direction by Rita Marshall

Photos by AP/Wide World, NBA Photos, Brian Spurlock

Library of Congress Cataloging-in-Publication Data

Nichols, John, 1966- The history of the Atlanta Hawks / by John Nichols.

p. cm. — (Pro basketball today)   ISBN 1-58341-090-2   1. Atlanta Hawks (Basketball team)—History—

Juvenile literature. [1. Atlanta Hawks (Basketball team)—History. 2. Basketball—History.] I. Title. II. Series.

GV885.52.A7 N53 2001   796.323′64′09758231—dc21   00-064542

First Edition 9 8 7 6 5 4 3 2 1

ATLANTA, GEORGIA, IS A VIBRANT CITY WITH A LONG HISTORY OF OVERCOMING OBSTACLES. FOUNDED IN THE

1830s, the city was built at the southern tip of the rugged Appalachian

Mountains, making it a gateway to the West for railroads and settlers. By

the start of the Civil War, Atlanta had grown into the Southeast's center

for industry and transportation. It had also become a stronghold of the

Confederate army.

In 1864, the Union army captured Atlanta and put it to the torch,

and a raging fire reduced the young city to ashes. Many people thought

that Atlanta would never recover, but the city gradually rebuilt. Today,

CLIFF HAGAN

Atlanta is home to a professional basketball team that has had its share of glorious triumphs and terrible defeats as well. That team, the Atlanta Hawks of the National Basketball Association (NBA), was born in 1949.

{AN NBA ORIGINAL} The Hawks franchise was originally known as the Tri-City Blackhawks, one of the NBA's 17 original teams. The team was shared by three neighboring cities in the Midwest: Rock Island, Illinois, Moline, Illinois, and Davenport, Iowa.

The Blackhawks spent two mediocre seasons in the Tri-Cities area before team owner Ben Kerner decided to move the club to Milwaukee, Wisconsin. There, a new 10,000-seat arena promised to lure fans in and give the team a financial boost. Kerner also decided to shorten the team's name to the Hawks.

SPUD WEBB

Bob Pettit averaged a stellar 26 points per game during his Hawks career.

BOB PETTIT

In their new home, the Hawks did draw bigger crowds, but their

fortunes on the court did not improve. Four straight losing seasons in

Milwaukee soured the fans, and in 1955, Kerner moved

his team again, this time to St. Louis, Missouri. The city

seemed to bring good luck to the franchise, and at long

last, the Hawks started to win.

The team was led by a 6-foot-9 and 240-pound for-

ward named Bob Pettit. Pettit was drafted out of Louisiana State in

1954 and had an immediate impact on the league. An explosive scorer

and ferocious rebounder, Pettit emerged as the Hawks' first true super-

star. In his first season, he was named the NBA Rookie of the Year. In

his second, Pettit averaged 25 points and 16 rebounds per game to earn

the league's Most Valuable Player award.

By the late '50s, the Hawks had surrounded Pettit with big-time

Scrappy point guard Slater "Dugie" Martin was one of the Hawks' top defenders in the late **'50s**.

SLATER MARTIN

Like Bob Pettit, Dikembe Mutombo was a dominant low-post defender.

DIKEMBE MUTOMBO

talent. Players such as forwards Cliff Hagan and Ed Macauley gave the team the look of a champion. In 1957, St. Louis drove all the way to the

Lenny Wilkens, who would later return as coach, was a five-time All-Star with the Hawks.

NBA Finals, only to lose to the powerful Boston Celtics in seven hard-fought games.

But the next season, the Hawks and Pettit would not be denied, capping a 41–31 regular season by defeating the mighty Celtics four games to two in the NBA Finals.

12 Pettit scored an incredible 50 points in the deciding sixth game to seal the franchise's first championship, 110–109.

The Hawks remained a contender through the early 1960s. New stars such as point guard Lenny Wilkens and center Clyde Lovellette were added to the lineup, but the team never regained the championship magic of 1958. After the 1964–65 season, Pettit retired. Five years later, the 11-time All-Star was inducted into the Basketball Hall of Fame.

CLYDE LOVELLETTE

{MOVING TO ATLANTA} The Hawks continued playing in St.

Louis until 1968, when Kerner decided to sell the team to a group of

Atlanta businessmen. The sale came as a shock to both cities, but Kerner

felt that St. Louis could no longer compete financially as an NBA market.

The move to Atlanta was made smoother by the emergence of

young star Lou Hudson. Nicknamed "Sweet Lou" by teammates and fans because of his shooting skill, the 6-foot-5 forward was deadly accurate from all over the court. "As soon as Lou steps in the gym, he's in range," joked Hawks forward Bill Bridges.

Hudson averaged more than 18 points a game during a stellar rookie year in 1966–67. Starting in 1968–69, Sweet Lou then led the Hawks to the playoffs for five straight seasons. But despite Hudson's efforts and those of other great players such as forward Zelmo Beaty and guards Walt Hazzard, Pete Maravich, and Joe "Pogo" Caldwell, the Hawks could not get past the second round of postseason play.

Part of the problem was that Atlanta kept losing talented players to the rival American Basketball Association (ABA). "We'd just get a good bunch together and then we'd lose one or two of them," complained Hawks head coach Richie Guerin after losing Beaty and

Pete Maravich, known as "Pistol Pete," thrilled fans with his flashy passing and shooting.

PETE MARAVICH

Caldwell in successive seasons.

After the Boston Celtics eliminated the Hawks in the second

round of the 1973 playoffs, Atlanta's postseason run was over. Four

straight losing seasons followed, leavings fans with little to cheer about

except Hudson's scoring exploits. Sweet Lou led the charge until 1977,

when he was traded to the Los Angeles Lakers.

The losing seasons of

the mid-1970s were hard on the Hawks franchise. Financial problems

accompanied the team's problems on the court, and it

was widely rumored that the Hawks would be forced to

move yet again.

All talk of another move was put to rest in January

1977, however, when Ted Turner bought the Hawks and

promised to keep them in Atlanta. Turner, a wealthy media mogul who

also owned professional baseball's Atlanta Braves, provided the stability

that the franchise needed to improve.

With the Hawks' financial problems behind them, the team's for-

tunes began to rise. In the 1977 NBA Draft, Atlanta chose 7-foot-1 and

250-pound center Wayne "Tree" Rollins. The towering Rollins gave the

team a fearsome defensive presence under the basket. "Tree is the type

Shot-block-
ing specialist
Tree Rollins
swatted
away 2,283
shots in 11
seasons in
Atlanta.

17

TREE ROLLINS

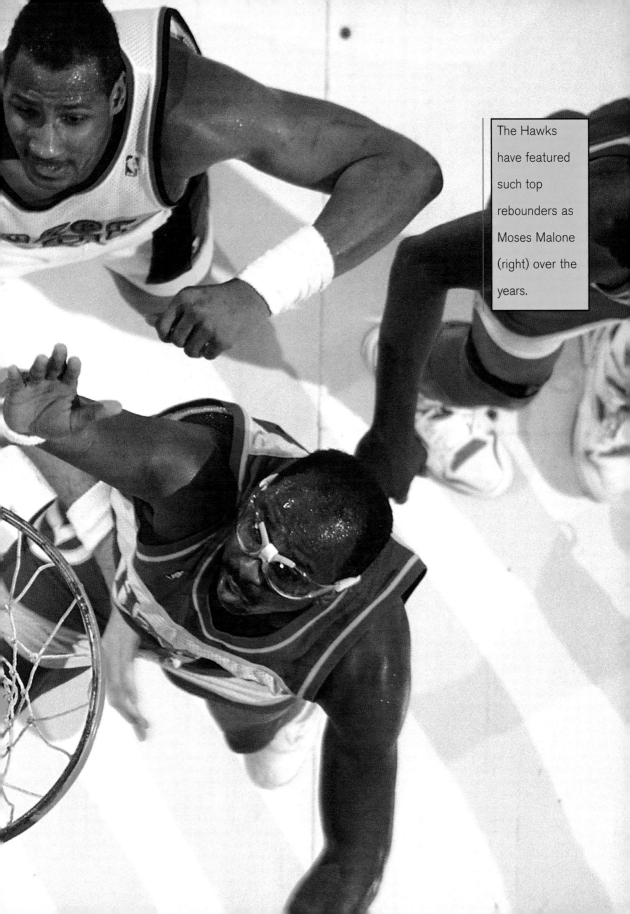

The Hawks have featured such top rebounders as Moses Malone (right) over the years.

of guy you hope to have around for 10 years," noted Hawks head coach

Hubie Brown. "He has a great work ethic and gives you everything he

has every night."

The Hawks also added 5-foot-8 point guard Charlie

Criss the same year. Often overlooked because of his size,

Criss had spent several years playing in various minor

leagues. In his rookie year with the Hawks, he was already

28 years old. But Criss quickly proved any doubters wrong by becoming

Atlanta's spark plug off the bench. "Charlie's speed and toughness

change the pace of the game," noted Coach Brown.

With these new additions to the lineup, the Hawks improved their

record to 41–41 and made the 1978 playoffs. Although Atlanta was

quickly eliminated by the Washington Bullets, the new Hawks were

clearly on the rise.

Forward Dan Roundfield averaged at least 15 points and 10 rebounds per game for five straight years.

DAN ROUNDFIELD

Throughout the early 1980s, Rollins, Criss, and power forward Dan

Roundfield formed the core of some good—if not great—Atlanta teams.

Although the Hawks were always sound defensively, they lacked the

scoring punch necessary to win big playoff games.

{THE "HUMAN HIGHLIGHT FILM"} On September 3, 1982,

the Hawks made a trade that would change the course of their history.

Atlanta dealt veteran forwards John Drew and Freeman Williams to the Utah Jazz for the draft rights to University of Georgia standout

Powerful for-
ward Kevin
Willis pulled
down 7,256
rebounds in
nine full
seasons with
Atlanta.

Dominique Wilkins.

The trade gave the Hawks the marquee offensive star they had been lacking. During his college career at Georgia, the high-flying Wilkins had earned the nickname the "Human Highlight Film" for his thrill-a-minute style

and sensational dunks, and he wasted no time making his mark in Atlanta. In his rookie year, the 6-foot-8 and 215-pound forward averaged 17 points a game.

To support Wilkins, the Hawks brought in several other key players over the next few years. By 1986, head coach Mike Fratello had surrounded Wilkins with such impressive performers as guards Anthony "Spud" Webb and Glenn "Doc" Rivers and bruising power forward Kevin Willis.

KEVIN WILLIS

Forward Dominique Wilkins was one of the most exciting scorers in NBA history.

DOMINIQUE WILKINS

In 1986–87, this new Hawks lineup posted a franchise-best 57–25 record. Leading the way, of course, was Wilkins, who finished second in the league in scoring with 29 points a game. "I think we will go as far as Dominique will carry us," noted Fratello.

In the 1987 playoffs, the Hawks soared past the Indiana Pacers in the first round to earn a showdown with the Detroit Pistons and their star point guard, Isiah Thomas. The two Eastern Conference powers slugged it out for five games, with the Hawks coming up short.

The next season, Coach Fratello guided the Hawks to another 50-win season, and again his team battled into the second round of the playoffs. This time Atlanta's opponent was the mighty Boston Celtics, led by forward Larry Bird. Fans were treated to a thrilling show as Wilkins and Bird staged a classic shootout, but in the end, the Celtics

Versatile guard Doc Rivers helped the Hawks fly high in **1986–87** with 10 assists per game.

DOC RIVERS

triumphed in a grueling seven-game series.

Wilkins's Human Highlight Film continued its run in Atlanta

through the 1993–94 season, when new coach Lenny Wilkens decided

to rebuild the team with younger players. In February 1994, Atlanta bid

farewell to Wilkins, who was traded to the Los Angeles Clippers for for-

ward Danny Manning.

{MUTOMBO MANS THE MIDDLE} In an effort to find the right combination of youth and athleticism, the Hawks continued to retool their lineup over the next few seasons. New players such as guards Steve Smith and Mookie Blaylock took center stage in Coach Wilkens's revamped attack.

Perhaps the biggest highlight of Atlanta's 1994–95 season was Wilkens's 939th coaching victory, which came against the Washington Bullets. With the win, he surpassed the legendary Arnold "Red" Auerbach of the Boston Celtics as the NBA's winningest coach. In 22 seasons of coaching in Seattle, Portland, Cleveland, and Atlanta, Wilkens proved to be as talented a coach as he was a player. In 1988, he had become only the second person (after the great John Wooden) to be inducted into the Basketball Hall of Fame as both a player and a coach.

After Wilkins's departure, Steve Smith emerged as the Hawks' top scorer in the late **'90s**.

STEVE SMITH

Despite Wilkens's brilliant leadership, the team made little

progress in the playoffs. Year after year, the Hawks' lack of a talented big

man left them vulnerable to inside attacks.

"Championship teams start from the inside out," noted

Wilkens. "We need a stronger presence down low in order

to contend."

Wilkens got his wish in 1996 when the Hawks signed

veteran center Dikembe Mutombo. The 7-foot-2 and 260-pound

Mutombo had already established himself as one of the game's most

daunting shot blockers and rebounders. In his first five seasons with the

Denver Nuggets, Mutombo had averaged more than 12 points, 12

rebounds, and 3 blocked shots a game. "He's an intimidator," said for-

ward Alan Henderson, another new addition to the Atlanta lineup.

"Now he's our intimidator."

MOOKIE BLAYLOCK

{SOARING INTO THE FUTURE} "Mount Mutombo," as fans nicknamed him, instantly became the linchpin of a much-improved Hawks team. Still, three winning seasons (from 1996–97 to 1998–99) were followed by three early exits in the playoffs. The Hawks were again tough defensively, but they lacked the offensive punch necessary to be a champion. In 1999, both Smith and Blaylock left the team. A year later, after the Hawks dropped to 28–54, Lenny Wilkens resigned as coach. It was time to rebuild again.

Forward Christian Laettner helped the Hawks win their first 11 games in **1997–98**.

Wilkens was replaced by Lon Kruger, formerly the head coach at the University of Illinois. Atlanta also made a key roster change late in 2000–01, trading the veteran Mutombo to Philadelphia for swingman Toni Kukoc and young shot blocker Theo Ratliff. Leading a lineup that included these players and guard Jason Terry, young forward DerMarr

CHRISTIAN LAETTNER

Veteran forward Alan Henderson steadied the Hawks during their rebuilding years.

ALAN HENDERSON

With great speed and ball-handling ability, young guard Jason Terry was a rising star.

JASON TERRY

Johnson, and point guard Brevin Knight, Coach Kruger was eager to rebuild the Hawks into a contender. "This organization is committed to building a winner, and by winner I mean a world champion," proclaimed Kruger. "Everything we do will be a step toward that goal."

For more than 50 years, the Hawks have been one of the NBA's most colorful franchises. They have enjoyed moments of glory, including one league title, and they have suffered setbacks. After some low times, today's Hawks hope to rebound like their hometown and once again fly to championship heights.

Fans hoped that forward DerMarr Johnson would become the next Dominique Wilkins.

DERMARR JOHNSON